RHODE ISLAND

RHODE ISLAND

HELLO
U.S.A.

by J. F. Warner

Lerner Publications Company

You'll find this picture of quahogs at the beginning of each chapter in this book. The quahog is a large hard-shell clam that lives in the ocean waters along Rhode Island. Quahogs were first introduced as food to Rhode Island settlers by Narragansett Indians. In 1987 Rhode Islanders chose the quahog as their official state shell.

Cover (left): The Breakers mansion in Newport. Cover (right): *Spirit of Rhode Island* sailing near Newport. Pages 2–3: Downtown Providence. Page 3: Blue violets.

This book is available in two editions:
Library binding by Lerner Publications Company, a division of Lerner Publishing Group
Soft cover by First Avenue Editions, an imprint of Lerner Publishing Group
241 First Avenue North
Minneapolis, MN 55401 U.S.A.

Website address: www.lernerbooks.com

Library of Congress Cataloging-in-Publication Data

Warner, J. F. (John F.)
    Rhode Island / J. F. Warner (Rev. and expanded 2nd ed.)
       p.   cm. — (Hello U.S.A.)
    Summary: An introduction to the geography, history, economy, people, environmental issues, and interesting sites of Rhode Island.
    Includes index.
    ISBN: 0–8225–4108–4 (lib. bdg. : alk paper)
    ISBN: 0–8225–0793–5 (pbk. : alk paper)
    1. Rhode Island—Juvenile literature. [1. Rhode Island.] I. Title. II. Series.
F79.3.W37 2003
974.5—dc21   2002008894

Manufactured in the United States of America
1 2 3 4 5 6 – JR – 08 07 06 05 04 03

CONTENTS

Narragansett Bay is a playground for boats of many shapes and sizes.

THE LAND

Little Rhody

ood things come in small packages."
Whoever thought up that old saying
could well have had Rhode Island in mind.
Rhode Island is just 59 miles long and 40 miles
wide. A person can take an unhurried tour of the
entire state in a single day! Travelers who do will
discover a greater variety of scenery than they might
expect to find in the smallest state in the country.

Rhode Island has rivers, lakes and ponds, farms
and forests, rolling hills, sandy beaches, bustling
cities, and quiet villages. And Narragansett Bay is
no more than a 30-minute drive from anywhere in
the state. An inlet of the Atlantic Ocean,
Narragansett Bay is sprinkled with islands of many
sizes and descriptions.

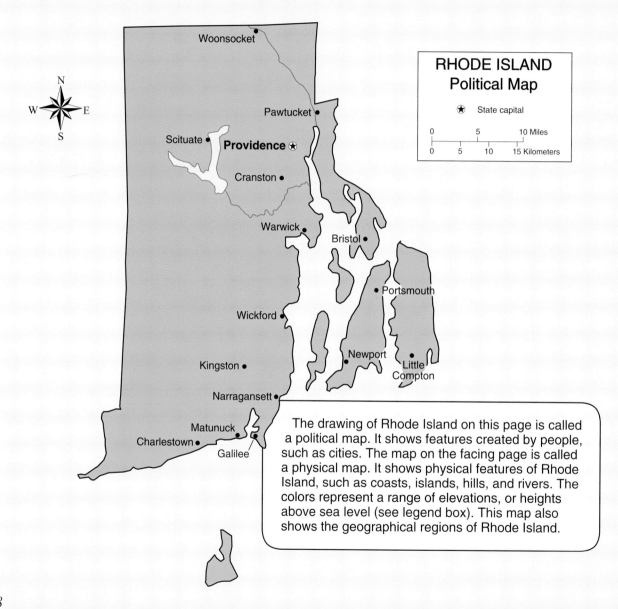

RHODE ISLAND
Political Map

★ State capital

0   5   10 Miles
0   5   10   15 Kilometers

Woonsocket

Pawtucket

Scituate •   **Providence** ☆

Cranston •

Warwick •

Bristol •

Portsmouth

Wickford •

Kingston •

Newport •   Little
            Compton

Narragansett •

Matunuck •

Charlestown •
    Galilee

The drawing of Rhode Island on this page is called a political map. It shows features created by people, such as cities. The map on the facing page is called a physical map. It shows physical features of Rhode Island, such as coasts, islands, hills, and rivers. The colors represent a range of elevations, or heights above sea level (see legend box). This map also shows the geographical regions of Rhode Island.

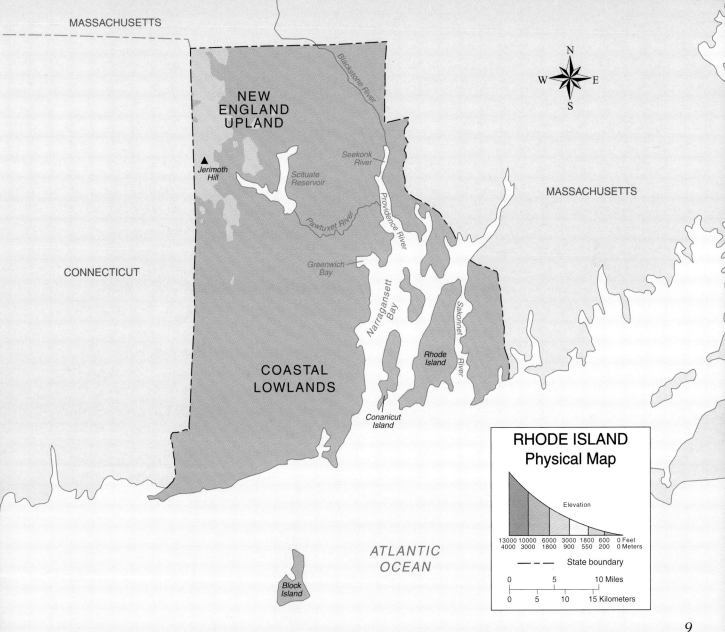

MASSACHUSETTS

NEW
ENGLAND
UPLAND

▲
*Jerimoth
Hill*

Blackstone River

*Seekonk
River*

*Scituate
Reservoir*

Pawtuxet River

Providence River

CONNECTICUT

MASSACHUSETTS

*Greenwich
Bay*

*Narragansett
Bay*

*Sakonnet
River*

*Rhode
Island*

COASTAL
LOWLANDS

*Conanicut
Island*

N
W   E
S

ATLANTIC
OCEAN

*Block
Island*

RHODE ISLAND
Physical Map

Elevation

| 13000 | 10000 | 6000 | 3000 | 1800 | 600 | 0 Feet |
| 4000 | 3000 | 1800 | 900 | 550 | 200 | 0 Meters |

- - -   State boundary

| 0 | | 5 | | 10 Miles |

| 0 | 5 | 10 | | 15 Kilometers |

Rhode Island and the other New England states are well known for forested hillsides that burst with bright fall colors.

Rhode Island is one of six states in a region of the northeastern United States known as New England. Tucked into the southeastern corner of New England, Rhode Island is bordered on the north and east by Massachusetts and on the west by Connecticut. The waters of the Atlantic Ocean form Rhode Island's southern boundary.

Rhode Island has two main land regions. One is the Coastal Lowlands in the south and east. The other is the New England Upland in the northwest. Both regions were formed by the **glaciers** that covered much of North America thousands of years ago. As these huge blocks of ice and snow crept down from the north, they carried sand and clay with them. When the glaciers finally melted, they left ridges of dirt and rock, called **moraines.**

The larger of the two regions, the Coastal Lowlands covers nearly two-thirds of Rhode Island. The region includes much of the mainland, all the islands in Narragansett Bay, and the lands bordering Massachusetts. Rhode Island's largest cities and most of its people are found in the Coastal Lowlands.

Block Island lies about 10 miles off of the mainland. The island is part of Rhode Island's Coastal Lowlands region.

The shores of Rhode Island's lowlands are marked by sandy beaches and numerous salt ponds and **lagoons** (shallow lakes or ponds). Rocky cliffs overlook Narragansett Bay from the coast and from many of its islands.

The Coastal Lowlands region rises in height until it meets the New England Upland. The upland begins where the land reaches a height of 200 feet above sea level. The region continues on up to 812 feet at Jerimoth Hill—the highest point in the state. Small towns, farms, and forests dot the New England Upland.

The New England Upland features many scenic lakes. Here, autumn comes to Spring Lake in northern Rhode Island.

Scituate Reservoir supplies water for Providence and other communities.

Rhode Island's largest inland body of water is Scituate Reservoir. This **reservoir,** or artificial lake, was made to store water for the capital city of Providence. The city and its surrounding communities get their water through a series of underground pipes leading from Scituate to individual homes and businesses.

The Blackstone, the Sakonnet, and the Pawtuxet are among the state's chief rivers. The Blackstone River begins in northeastern Rhode Island and flows southward. It is renamed the Seekonk and then the Providence River before reaching Narragansett Bay. The Pawtuxet River flows from Scituate Reservoir into the Providence River.

Despite Rhode Island's northern location, the state's climate is mild. January temperatures average 29° F. In July temperatures average 71° F. **Precipitation** (rain, snow, sleet, and hail) averages 44 inches a year. More than half of this moisture falls in the form of snow, mostly in the New England Upland.

These young Rhode Islanders are prepared for the state's winter weather.

Hurricanes sometimes pound the coastal areas, leaving beaches and even roads in ruins.

A destructive form of weather—hurricanes—sometimes affects Rhode Island. Over the years, the strong winds and heavy rains created by these damaging coastal storms have hit the state many times. Hurricane season runs from June to November.

Apple blossoms *(right)* bloom in the spring in Rhode Island. Red foxes *(below)* roam Rhode Island's forests.

More than half of Rhode Island is forested, and trees are one of the state's most valuable resources. Some of the most common trees include ash, birch, cedar, oak, pine, and, of course, the state's official tree—the red maple. Wild plants such as dogwoods, mountain laurels, rhododendrons, and violets add delicate touches of color in the spring.

Numerous streams and ponds help support many kinds of wildlife in the state's forests. Deer, foxes, and mink abound, as do game birds such as partridges, pheasants, wild turkeys, and quail.

Fighting for Freedom

As long as 10,000 years ago, people were living in the part of North America that came to be known as New England. Little is known about these early Native Americans, or Indians. We do know that by the 1500s, about 30,000 descendants of the early Indians were living in five tribes located throughout the Rhode Island region.

The largest and most powerful of these tribes was the Narragansett, who made up at least half of the area's population. They shared the area with the Wampanoag, the Nipmuck, the Niantic, and the Pequot.

During a special ceremony, the Narragansett Indians smoked tobacco in a long, feathered pipe.

Narragansett Indians were living in the Rhode Island area by the 1500s. Narragansett Bay provided flounder and shellfish.

These Native Americans were farmers, hunters, and fishers. In the winter, the Indians lived in a longhouse that could hold up to 20 families. During the summer, they lived in wigwams—homes supported by poles covered with tree bark or animal skins. The Indians used beads as money. They passed stories and knowledge from generation to generation by word of mouth.

Each village had a judge who sentenced criminals according to a fixed set of rules. Tribe members liked to compete in running and swimming, and they played a game something like American football.

No one knows for sure which group of Europeans first visited what later became Rhode Island. Some people believe it was the Vikings, from Scandinavia. Others say the Portuguese were first. In any event, the first real evidence comes from the writings of Giovanni da Verrazzano. He was an Italian explorer who explored the Narragansett Bay area in 1524 and described it in his diary.

Rhode Island's Old Stone Mill in Newport is a mystery. Some people think the Vikings built it more than one thousand years ago. Other people believe the mill dates from the early 1600s.

ADRIAEN BLOCK
ANº 1614

Block Island is named for Dutch sailor Adriaen Block, who explored Rhode Island's coast in the early 1600s.

Verrazzano was later followed by Adriaen Block, a Dutch sailor who arrived in the bay in 1614. Neither Verrazzano nor Block had planned to bring settlers from his home country to live near Narragansett Bay. The British would be the first to do that.

In Great Britain in the early 1600s, the Church of England and the government were practically one and the same. Those who did not follow the laws of the church were punished severely by the government. Sometimes they were thrown in jail or even put to death. Some people fled Great Britain to practice the religion of their choice.

The Puritans, a religious group that wanted to "purify" the Church of England, left Britain in the early 1600s. They sailed across the Atlantic Ocean to North America, where they founded the Massachusetts Bay Colony in the Massachusetts area.

In the **colony,** residents, or colonists, still thought of themselves as British citizens and obeyed the orders of the British king. But in their faraway colony, the Puritans could change the rules of the church without being punished.

Roger Williams, a Puritan minister, left England in 1630 with his wife and newborn daughter. They sailed to Boston, the center of the Massachusetts Bay Colony, with high hopes of having true freedom of religion. Their hopes were soon dashed, however. The Puritans had their religious freedom but demanded that everyone who joined the colony follow the beliefs of the Puritan church.

Williams's religious views differed somewhat from those of the Puritans in Massachusetts. He fled the colony soon after learning that the Puritans were planning to send him back to Britain because of his beliefs.

Roger Williams founded Providence, the first permanent white settlement in Rhode Island.

Williams headed south to a spot near Narragansett Bay. In 1636 he founded the city of Providence on land given to him by the Narragansett Indians, with whom he had made friends. Then he invited any and all to join him in his new city. Baptists, Quakers, Jews, people of no religion—all were welcome.

Eventually, new settlements grew up around Providence. The Puritans in Massachusetts Bay tried to gain control of them. Under the Puritans, the religious freedoms enjoyed by the settlers would be lost. Alarmed, Roger Williams set sail for Britain to convince King Charles II to stop the Puritans.

The people of Providence were free to worship in the church of their choice—a freedom people in the Massachusetts Bay Colony and in Great Britain did not have.

In 1643 soldiers from Massachusetts surrounded the home of Samuel Gorton in Warwick, a town near Providence. Gorton had committed a crime by setting foot in Massachusetts after leaders had banned him years earlier for his religious beliefs. Gorton was taken to Massachusetts, where he was sentenced to six months hard labor before being allowed to return to Warwick.

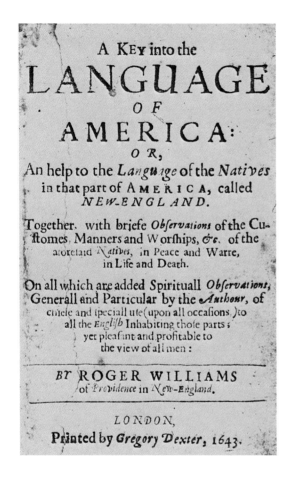

A KEY into the
LANGUAGE
OF
AMERICA:
OR,
An help to the *Language* of the *Natives* in that part of A M E R I C A, called *NEW-ENGLAND.*

Together. with briefe *Observations* of the Cu-ftomes, Manners and Worſhips, &c. of the aforeſaid *Natives*, in Peace and Warre, in Life and Death.

On all which are added Spirituall *Obſervations,* Generall and Particular by the *Authour*, of chiefe and ſpeciall uſe (upon all occaſions)to all the *Engliſh* Inhabiting thoſe parts ; yet pleaſant and profitable to the view of all men :

BY ROGER WILLIAMS *of Providence in New-England.*

LONDON,
Printed by *Gregory Dexter*, 1643.

Roger Williams learned to speak the Narragansett language and even wrote a book about it.

In 1644 the king gave Williams a **charter,** or written permission, to establish the Providence Plantations in Narragansett Bay. With this charter, Providence and its nearby plantations, or settlements, became an official colony of Great Britain.

The new colony was an equal of Massachusetts Bay and was protected by the king. So Williams and the others were free to worship as they pleased.

Meanwhile, more people began leaving Britain to live in North America. Like Williams, some of these settlers were looking for a place to practice their religion. Others wanted to farm or to trade with the Indians. In total, the newcomers established 13 colonies along the East Coast. Colonies in what became the northeastern United States were called New England.

The Road to Rhode

In 1663 a second charter gave the colony a new name—the Colony of Rhode Island and Providence Plantations. The colonists soon shortened it to, simply, Rhode Island. Rhode Island was the name of Narragansett Bay's largest island, which up until 1644 had been called Aquidneck. (To avoid confusion, some people still say Aquidneck when referring to the island of Rhode Island.)

No one is quite sure where the name Rhode Island comes from. Some people credit Giovanni da Verrazzano, who wrote in 1524 that the island reminded him of the Greek island of Rhodes, in the Aegean Sea. Others believe that the Dutch sailor Adriaen Block, noting the red earth along the island's shoreline, called the place Roodt Eylandt, which means "red island" in Dutch.

Giovanni da Verrazzano

More and more people sailed the ocean to settle in New England and the other colonies. The colonists were not interested in sharing the land with the Indians who lived there, and the Indians became angry. Often, colonists simply took land from the Indians to build homes and to raise crops.

In 1675 Metacomet (called King Philip by the colonists), chief of the Wampanoag, went to war against the New England colonists. Metacomet and his supporters wanted to regain their homeland. The major battle of King Philip's War was fought in Rhode Island. On December 19, 1675, about 500 Wampanoag and Narragansett were killed in the Great Swamp Fight near Kingston, Rhode Island. Many of the Indians who survived were sold into slavery.

Less than a year after the war began, Metacomet was tracked down and killed. Without Metacomet's leadership, Native Americans in the New England

In 1676 an Indian ally of the settlers killed Metacomet.

Rhode Island became famous for the Narragansett Pacer.

colonies became almost powerless. The Indians lost King Philip's War in 1678. In Rhode Island, the Native Americans still left were given a small plot of land on which to live.

Throughout the 1700s, Rhode Islanders turned more and more to the sea for wealth. Providence, Newport, and Bristol became bustling seaports. Rhode Islanders built vessels for hunting whales. The large sea animals were caught for their blubber, or fat, which was cooked into an oil. The colony's fleet of merchant ships carried milk, cheese, wood, and the Narragansett Pacer—a famous breed of horse—to other parts of the world.

From Rum to Riches

In the 1700s, the colonists of Rhode Island dabbled in what became known as the triangular trade and soon discovered wealth beyond anyone's imagination.

For Rhode Islanders, the triangular trade involved three ports and three cargoes. It began in Newport, where merchant ships were loaded with kegs of rum. The rum was shipped to West Africa, where it was traded for Africans. The Africans were shipped to the West Indies to be sold into slavery in exchange for molasses, sugar, and money.

Then came the last stage and the completion of the triangle. The ships returned to the colonies, where the remaining Africans were sold into slavery. The sugar and molasses from the West Indies were used to make more rum, which was used to buy more African slaves.

The trade went on and on, and the colonists made huge profits. At the time, the cost of making rum was about 25 cents a gallon. Merchants could buy slaves in Africa for about 200 gallons of rum, or $50. Slaves sold in the colonies for up to $400 each. Rhode Island outlawed the slave trade in 1774.

The British king wanted Rhode Islanders and other colonists to rely on Great Britain for some of their goods. He decided to make it difficult for colonists to make a profit on their own goods. He created new taxes and refused to allow the colonists to make certain products, such as iron goods and cloth.

The colonists disliked these and other laws. They wanted to govern themselves and make their own laws. In 1775 the 13 colonies joined together to fight for their freedom as an independent nation.

Rhode Island saw few battles during the American War of Independence, but Rhode Islanders fought hard for their freedom. Two Rhode Islanders led the Continental, or colonial, troops. Esek Hopkins *(top)* of Providence served as commander in chief of the Continental navy, and Nathanael Greene *(bottom)* of Warwick became a respected general in the Continental army.

On May 4, 1776, Rhode Island became the first colony to formally declare itself independent of Great Britain. On July 4, 1776, representatives from the colonies approved the Declaration of Independence, a letter stating that the colonies were officially free of British rule. With the signing of the Declaration of Independence, the United States of America was born. The colonists did not actually defeat the British until years later, in 1783.

The former 13 colonies could not become states of the Union until they approved the U.S. Constitution, or set of basic national laws. Although Rhode Island had been the first colony to declare independence, it was the last to formally approve the Constitution. On May 29, 1790, Rhode Island became the 13th state.

French troops landed in Newport in 1780. The French helped Continental forces throughout the colonies defeat the British.

Around this time, Moses Brown, a wealthy merchant from Providence, and Samuel Slater, a British textile worker, met in Pawtucket, Rhode Island. Slater had the plans to an invention that would change the United States forever.

In 1793 in Pawtucket, the two men built the country's first water-powered cotton mill. This event was the beginning of the **Industrial Revolution** in the United States. For the first time in U.S. history, people left their spinning wheels at home and went to work in factories, where products such as cloth could be made much faster. Since working the machinery required little practice, even people unskilled in the making of cloth could work in the factory.

By 1840 Rhode Island's population had grown to more than 100,000. Waves of **immigrants**— including children—arrived to work in the many cotton and woolen mills in the state. First came the Irish, then the French Canadians and Swedes, followed by Poles, Greeks, and Russians. Later came the Portuguese, Chinese, and Italians.

Some mill workers stood during their entire 14-hour workdays.

Thread and Water

By the late 1700s, the British had developed water-powered machines that produced certain goods quickly and efficiently, spurring industrial growth in Great Britain. Spinning machines for making thread and yarn were among these inventions. To make sure other countries did not profit from these powerful tools, Britain made it illegal to take any machines—or the plans or models to make them—out of the country. Even the people who worked with the machines were not allowed to leave the country.

Disguised as a farmer, textile worker Samuel Slater escaped from central England and traveled to America. From memory he re-created the water-powered spinning machines developed by Richard Arkwright in Britain. The machines poured out cotton yarn at speeds faster than Americans had ever seen. Slater opened a cotton mill, or factory, in Pawtucket. Before long, the number of factories using water-powered machinery had multiplied, and the American Industrial Revolution was born.

Despite Rhode Island's growth, its government had fallen far behind the times. The charter of 1663, still the supreme law of Rhode Island, awarded voting rights only to male landowners and their eldest sons. In the mid-1800s, less than 40 percent of the state's population had a say in government.

Thomas W. Dorr, a fiery activist, wanted to change the outdated voting law. In 1842 he started what became known as the Dorr Rebellion. Dorr's followers were the landless, many of whom were immigrants. Dorr and his supporters wrote a new state constitution that gave more people the right to vote, and then they held their own elections.

Dorr formed an army and tried to take over the state government by force. The rebellion failed, and Dorr left Rhode Island. Some of Dorr's ideas about voting, however, were accepted in a new state constitution passed in 1843.

In 1842 some Rhode Islanders elected activist Thomas Dorr as governor of Rhode Island. The state government never recognized Dorr's title because the election was unofficial.

GOVERNOR DORR

GOVERNOR DORR

CIGARS
EXTRA * FINE

Rhode Island became a fashionable summer vacation place for the rich in the late 1800s and early 1900s. Many wealthy people built large mansions along the coast.

In the late 1800s, the sea was still important to Rhode Island. The U.S. Navy opened a base in Newport in 1883. Whaling, shipbuilding, and fishing flourished. At the same time, Rhode Island's farming industry was weakening. As the state's population grew, companies bought land from farmers to build housing for mill workers and their families. Many farmers, whose incomes depended on how well their crops did, left their fields to work in the mills for steady wages.

The navy's presence in Rhode Island continued to grow. In 1883 the Newport Naval Station began docking large ships in Narragansett Bay's deep-water ports. In 1884 the Naval War College started training students in naval military tactics. During World War I (1914–1918), shipyards in the bay area built combat boats. During World War II (1939–1945), the navy opened the Quonset Point Naval Air Station in 1941, and the entire bay area became a beehive of naval activity.

After the war ended in 1945, the navy remained, but many of the warships were taken to other ports. Wartime industries, such as electronics and plastics, changed the products they made. These types of factories replaced many of the cotton and woolen mills that had moved to the southern states, where the mills were much cheaper to operate.

During World War II, labor shortages prompted many women to enter the workforce. In Newport, factory workers made torpedoes for the navy.

Since 1884 the Naval War College in Newport has trained navy officers.

By the 1960s, the state had begun to encourage people from other states to vacation in Rhode Island, hoping to create jobs in hotels and restaurants. Visitors were able to reach the islands in Narragansett Bay more easily in 1969, when the Newport Bridge was completed. The bridge connects the island of Rhode Island with Conanicut Island.

New waves of immigrants in the 1970s and 1980s added to the state's ethnic mix. Puerto Ricans, Colombians, and Southeast Asians settled in the state.

The Newport Bridge, which is 2.5 miles long, was completed in 1969.

In 1991 a Rhode Island family wanted to turn their land over to people who would preserve the woods and swampland. They returned hundreds of acres of land to the Narragansett Indians.

In 1990 the Ocean State celebrated the bicentennial (200th anniversary) of its statehood. Soon after, the state's economy began to slump. A drop in manufacturing led to job losses. For the first time ever, population decreased, as people moved away in search of new jobs.

Rhode Islanders made efforts to turn the economy around, however, and by 1998 the economy was rebounding. New jobs in high-tech industries such as manufacturing scientific instruments and pharmaceuticals have helped strengthen the economy.

A growing tourism industry has also given Rhode Island a boost. In 2000 tourism brought in more than $3 billion to the state. Rhode Islanders are also working to make education a top priority, preparing their citizens for a bright future.

PEOPLE & ECONOMY

The Ocean State

 iving and working in Rhode Island means living and working in an ethnically mixed state. Most of the population can trace their roots back to various countries in Europe. About 8 percent of Rhode Island's population is Latino, and African Americans make up about 4 percent of the population. Asian Americans and Native Americans together make up less than 3 percent of the state's 1 million people.

The few thousand Native Americans in Rhode Island are mostly descendants of the Narragansett and the Wampanoag, who greeted the first European settlers more than 300 years ago.

Rhode Island's residents enjoy the Ocean State's 400 miles of coastline.

Nearly 174,000 people—about one-sixth of Rhode Island's population—live in Providence.

Living and working in Rhode Island also means being in one of the most crowded states in the nation. For each square mile of land, there are more than 1,000 persons. Of the 50 states, only New Jersey is more densely populated.

Nearly all Rhode Islanders—more than 90 percent—live in cities. Rhode Island's most populated city is Providence, the capital. Warwick, Cranston, and Pawtucket are other large cities in Rhode Island. All of these cities are near Narragansett Bay.

A residential section of Providence features tight clusters of homes.

Much of Providence is a living museum. Many of its parks and gardens, buildings, and homes date back to colonial days. Providence also boasts two world-famous schools—Brown University and the Rhode Island School of Design, each with museums of its own. The city has professional theater groups, an opera, and a ballet company.

Providence is not the only cultural center in Rhode Island. The village of Wickford on the shores of Narragansett Bay holds an art show that draws artists and art lovers from all across the country each year.

A student at the Rhode Island School of Design studies the paintings in the school's Museum of Art.

This Narragansett man displays some traditional Narragansett Indian beadwork.

The town of Matunuck on the Atlantic coast has a summer theater noted for its plays and musicals. In nearby Charlestown, on a **reservation** run by the Narragansett, Native Americans hold an annual fall festival. The weeklong event teaches visitors Narragansett history and traditions.

Newport is the home of numerous historical sites. Built in 1747, the Redwood Library is the oldest lending library still in use in the United States. The Old Stone Mill, a structure some people believe was built by the Vikings, may be more than a thousand years old. Newport also hosts jazz and folk festivals, as well as an international festival of classical music.

Newport's JVC Jazz Festival draws crowds of people *(right)* who come to hear performers such as Ray Charles *(above, playing the piano)*.

Windsurfers enjoy miles of waves in the waters of Rhode Island.

Rhode Island takes education seriously. One of the first public schools in the colonies was started in Newport in 1640. In 1800 Rhode Island became the first state in the Union to collect taxes to pay for public schools. Rhode Island spends more money per pupil than most other states.

Forests, the ocean, and the bay make Rhode Island a playground for those who love the outdoors. Twenty state parks provide swimming areas, campgrounds, hiking trails, and nature preserves. Sailing, snorkeling, fishing, ice-skating, and skiing can all be enjoyed in season.

Baseball fans cheer on the Pawtucket Red Sox—also known as the PawSox.

Sports fans can watch many competitions through-out the year. Rhode Island has professional tennis and golf matches, sailing races, boat shows, college sports, and an annual marathon. The state also cheers on the Pawtucket Red Sox—the top minor-league team of the professional Boston Red Sox baseball club.

About 67 percent of Rhode Island's workers are employed in service jobs. Service workers have jobs as doctors, sales clerks, bankers, waiters, and tour guides. Rhode Islanders who work for the U.S. government make up 13 percent of the workforce. The U.S. naval base in Newport employs thousands of workers, including engineers and clerks.

Newport Harbor docks U.S. Navy ships, such as this destroyer.

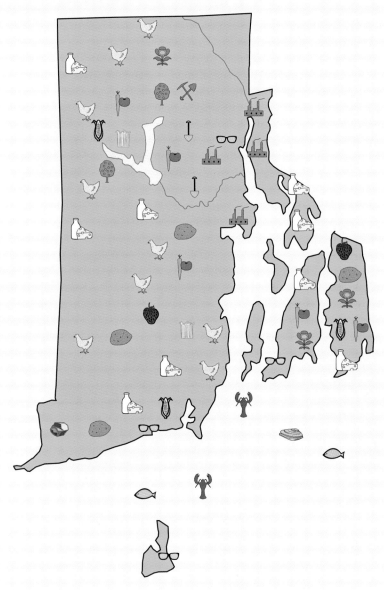

RHODE ISLAND
Economic Map

The symbols on this map show where different economic activities take place in Rhode Island. The legend below explains what each symbol stands for.

🍓	Berries	🦞	Lobsters
🦪	Clams	🏭	Manufacturing
🌽	Corn	🌼	Nursery products
🥛	Dairy products	🥔	Potatoes
🐟	Fish	🐔	Poultry
🌳	Fruit	⛏	Sand and gravel
🪨	Granite	⛏	Stone
🌾	Hay	👓	Tourism
	🥕	Vegetables	

Nearly 15 percent of Rhode Island's workers have jobs in manufacturing. The state is a leader in making jewelry and silverware. Both of these industries are centered in Providence. Rhode Islanders also make machinery, scientific tools, cloth, plastics, electrical equipment, and ships.

Agriculture employs 1 percent of Rhode Island's workforce. Out of all the agricultural goods produced in Rhode Island, shrubs and trees used for landscaping, Christmas trees, sod, and milk make the most money. Some of the sod, which is grown on special farms, is used to cover the playing fields of many sports stadiums in the northeastern United States.

Apples *(above)* and Christmas trees *(left)* are among Rhode Island's leading crops.

Rhode Island's fishing fleet has gotten smaller in the past few years, but fishing is still important to the state's economy. One reason for the industry's success is the high price people will pay for seafood. Another is that people around the world want to eat the fish caught in Rhode Island's waters. Tuna, striped bass, and flounder are the state's top catches.

Nets like these haul in fish and shellfish.

Fishing boats called trollers slowly tow several long fishing poles through the water.

Lobster ranks number one in Rhode Island's nets. Scallops are another important shellfish. Quahogs (hard-shell clams) are in demand wherever seafood lovers can be found. Finally, there is the menhaden catch. Menhaden, fish that are usually processed into fish oil or fertilizer, are caught in huge numbers each fall and winter. Ships from places as far away as Russia anchor in Narragansett Bay to buy the menhaden catch off Rhode Island's fishing boats.

THE ENVIRONMENT

Saving the Bay

arragansett Bay plays a large role in the lives of Rhode Islanders. The bay is a major source of food, yielding more than $165 million in lobster catches. Fish such as flounder are caught and sold by the ton. Fish and shellfish together bring in almost $600 million a year for Rhode Island.

The bay earns Rhode Island even more money from tourism and boating. Tourists spend more than $1.4 billion each year docking their boats, eating at restaurants, and shopping at stores on the bay.

Quahogs are thick-shelled clams that make up an important part of Rhode Island's fishing industry.

This shellfisher digs for quahogs with a bullrake—a long metal pole with a rakelike tool at one end.

Narragansett Bay is crucial to Rhode Island's economy.

This Rhode Island marina, or dock, fills with sailboats, speedboats, and yachts. Boating is a large part of the state's tourism industry.

Narragansett Bay is obviously important to Rhode Islanders, but sometimes it is not treated as well as you might expect. For more than 100 years, untreated sewage—waste carried by water through sinks and toilets—has been dumped into the bay.

Most of the time, the sewage is carried with **wastewater** through pipes to a sewage treatment plant. The plant removes solid matter from the wastewater. The plant then treats, or cleans, the wastewater before releasing it into the waters of Narragansett Bay.

Sewage and storm water flow through a combined sewer before rushing into Narragansett Bay.

Not all sewage, however, makes it to the sewage treatment plant. Some of Rhode Island's sewers are very old. They were built in the 1800s when Rhode Island's cities relied on **combined sewers**—that is, sewers that carry both sewage and storm water directly to the bay.

Cities have since added pipes to the combined sewers to channel both wastewater and storm water to treatment plants. But when there is a heavy rain, storm water fills up these pipes and eventually the treatment plant. When the treatment plant is completely full, any excess wastewater and storm water go untreated. The polluted water overflows straight into the bay, just as it did 100 years ago.

When untreated sewage overflows into the bay, officials must close beaches, fishing grounds, and shellfish beds for weeks—and sometimes months— at a time. The pollution greatly affects areas where fish or shellfish have their young. The damage costs the fishing and tourism industries millions of dollars every year.

Rhode Islanders are working to protect this valuable resource. In 1993 the Comprehensive Conservation and Management Plan (CCMP) was created to help improve water quality and to protect the bay. By identifying and monitoring pollution sources, the CCMP hopes to improve the quality of the bay.

Signs like this warn fishers that the water is polluted.

NO SHELLFISHING

POLLUTED AREA
Rhode Island Department of
Environmental Management

Organizations such as Save the Bay, which is dedicated to cleaning up Narragansett Bay, work with leaders of industry, with government officials, with ordinary citizens, and with schoolchildren. Save the Bay tries to keep people aware of what's happening in Narragansett Bay by sponsoring an annual swim across the bay, ferryboat rides, and educational programs. The group is also trying to get cities to spend the millions of dollars needed to control pollution from combined sewers.

Despite the efforts of Save the Bay and other groups, the problems of pollution in Narragansett

Rhode Island shellfishers protest against pollution in Narragansett Bay.

Members of Save the Bay educate students about the importance of marine life in the bay.

Bay have not all been solved. About 4 billion gallons of pollution still end up in the bay each year. Public beaches still shut down from time to time during the peak summer season. Thousands of acres of rich shellfish beds are sometimes closed to fishers for much of the year because of pollution in the bay.

Many people are working hard to help the bay. But all Rhode Islanders must do their share by making sure cities are doing all they can to avoid polluting Narragansett Bay. In a state such as Rhode Island—where people rely on the bay for food, jobs, and leisure—conquering pollution is everyone's business.

ALL ABOUT RHODE ISLAND

Fun Facts

Rhode Island, the nation's smallest state, has the longest official name—State of Rhode Island and Providence Plantations.

Some of the tuna fish caught in the waters off Rhode Island weigh nearly 1,000 pounds. That's enough to make 20,000 tuna fish sandwiches!

About 250 Rhode Islands could fit into the state of Texas. Because of its small size, Rhode Island is sometimes called Little Rhody.

Rhode Island's state bird is a chicken. The Rhode Island Red was first bred in Little Compton, Rhode Island, in 1854. The bird's plentiful eggs and tasty meat made it the chicken of choice for U.S. poultry farmers.

Rhode Island claims the nation's first public roller-skating rink (1866), first golf course (1890), and first automobile parade (1899).

The longest game in baseball history was played in the city of Pawtucket in 1981. The Pawtucket Red Sox and the Rochester Red Wings played 32 innings April 18 and 19. The teams were still tied at 2–2, so the game was resumed on June 23. In the 33rd inning, the PawSox finally won 3–2.

Rhode Island Red

STATE SONG

RHODE ISLAND IT'S FOR ME

Words by Charlie Hall; music by Maria Day; arranged by Kathryn Chester

*I've been to every state we have
and I think that I'm inclined to say
that Rhody stole my heart:
You can keep the forty-nine.*

*Herring gulls that dot the sky,
blue waves that paint the rocks,
waters rich with Neptune's life,
the boats that line the docks,
I see the lighthouse flickering
to help the sailors see.
There's a place for everyone:
Rhode Island it's for me.*

*Rhode Island, oh, Rhode Island
surrounded by the sea.
Some people roam the earth for home:
Rhode Island it's for me.*

You can hear "Rhode Island It's for Me" by visiting this website:
<http://www.50states.com/songs/rdisl.htm>

A RHODE ISLAND RECIPE

Apples are Rhode Island's most important fruit crop. Developed in 1796, Rhode Island greening apples keep their tart taste in cooking. If you can't find greening apples, other tart apples, such as Granny Smith, can be used instead. Ask an adult for help with all steps that use an oven.

APPLE CRISP

3 pounds tart apples
2 tablespoons lemon juice
½ cup brown sugar
½ teaspoon cinnamon
½ teaspoon nutmeg

⅓ cup all-purpose flour
⅓ cup granulated sugar
½ cup rolled oats
4 tablespoons cold butter
½ cup chopped walnuts or pecans

1. Have an adult help you peel, core, and chop apples. In a bowl, toss apples with lemon juice to prevent darkening.

2. In a separate bowl, combine brown sugar, cinnamon, and nutmeg. Stir mixture into apples. Set aside.

3. Combine flour, sugar, and oats in a separate bowl. Cut butter into 8 pieces. Mix butter into flour until mixture looks like crumbs. Stir in nuts.

4. Butter a 10 × 10-inch baking dish. Spread apples in bottom of dish. Sprinkle apples with flour mixture.

5. Bake at 375° for 45 minutes, or until apples are tender and topping is lightly browned.

Makes 8 servings.

HISTORICAL TIMELINE

8,000 B.C. Indians inhabit the Rhode Island area.

A.D. 1524 Giovanni da Verrazzano explores Narragansett Bay.

1614 Dutch explorer Adriaen Block arrives in Narragansett Bay.

1636 Roger Williams founds Providence.

1640 Rhode Island's first public school opens in Newport.

1644 An English charter unites the settlements of Providence, Portsmouth, Newport, and Warwick.

1663 The King of England grants Rhode Island a second charter.

1675–1678 Metacomet leads Wampanoag Indians in King Philip's War, an uprising against the colonists. The Indians are eventually defeated.

1774 Rhode Island becomes the first colony to outlaw the slave trade.

1776 Rhode Island declares its independence from British rule.

1790 The American Industrial Revolution begins in Pawtucket; Rhode Island becomes the 13th state.

1793 Samuel Slater and Moses Brown open the country's first water-powered cotton mill in Pawtucket.

1842 Outdated voting laws spark the Dorr Rebellion.

1843 Rhode Island passes a new state constitution, which gives more people the right to vote.

1883 The United States Navy opens a naval base in Newport.

1884 The Naval War College opens in Newport.

1941 Quonset Point Naval Air Station is established.

1969 Newport Bridge is completed.

1990 Rhode Island celebrates the 200th anniversary of its statehood.

1993 The Comprehensive Conservation and Management Plan (CCMP) is created to protect Narragansett Bay.

2000 Tourism brings in more than $3 billion to Rhode Island.

OUTSTANDING RHODE ISLANDERS

Edward Bannister (1828–1901) was an artist who lived in Providence. Bannister became one of the first African American artists to gain international fame. His most famous works include a painting entitled "Under the Oaks."

Emma Bugbee (1888–1981), a journalist and author, worked to gain rights for women. In 1911 she became the first female reporter to work in the city-news division of the *New York Herald Tribune.* Bugbee lived in Warwick.

Emma Bugbee

Ambrose Burnside (1824–1881), who lived in Bristol, became governor of Rhode Island after serving as a general for the Union army during the Civil War. Burnside's thick whiskers gave rise to the term *sideburns.*

Ambrose Burnside

Ruth Buzzi (born 1936) is an entertainer who has appeared on many television shows, including *Laugh-In* and *Sesame Street.* The comedienne from Westerly has won a Golden Globe Award and is a member of the Rhode Island Hall of Fame.

Marian Chace (1896–1970), of Providence, was a dancer and activist who applied dance as therapy for the mentally ill. In 1966 she founded the American Dance Therapy Association to promote the use of dance as therapy for all types of people.

Ruth Buzzi

George M. Cohan (1878–1942) wrote more than 40 plays and musicals. He also produced and starred in many of them. Cohan, who was from Providence, also wrote many popular songs, such as "Yankee Doodle Boy," "Over There," and "You're a Grand Old Flag."

George M. Cohan

Nicholas Colasanto (1924–1985) was a television and film actor from Providence. One of the last roles he played was the character of Coach Ernie Pantusso on the long-running television series *Cheers*.

Nicholas Colasanto

Bill Conti (born 1942) is a songwriter who wrote theme songs for such television series as *Dynasty*, *Falcon Crest*, and *Cagney and Lacey*. Conti, from Providence, has also written music scores for films, including *Rocky* and *The Right Stuff*.

Hugh Duffy (1866–1954), born in Cranston, was a professional baseball player. During his career, Duffy participated as player, manager, and executive. In 1945 he was named to the National Baseball Hall of Fame. Duffy still holds the all-time record for the highest single-season batting average (.440 in 1894).

Hugh Duffy

Jabez Gorham (1792–1869), a silversmith and businessman from Providence, founded Gorham Inc. in 1831. Gorham's was the first company to use machines to plate silver.

Robert Gray (1755–1806) was an explorer from Tiverton, Rhode Island. In 1790 he captained the first American ship to sail around the world.

Robert Gray

Spalding Gray (born 1941) is a writer, actor, and performer from Barrington, Rhode Island. Gray is known for his autobiographical monologues and the theater company the Wooster Group, which he co-founded in 1977. His works include *Swimming to Cambodia* and *Gray's Anatomy*.

David Hartman (born 1935) has worked in television as an actor, host, and producer. He is most commonly associated with ABC's talk show *Good Morning America*, which he co-hosted from 1975 to 1987. Hartman is from Pawtucket.

Spalding Gray

Matilda Jones

Napoleon "Larry" Lajoie

Ida Lewis

Princess Red Wing

Charles "Gabby" Hartnett (1900–1972) of Woonsocket was one of baseball's greatest catchers. Because of his rosy complexion and serious expression, Hartnett was nicknamed Old Tomato Face. He was named the National League's Most Valuable Player in 1935.

Stephen Hopkins (1707–1785) served as colonial governor of Rhode Island for eight years and was a member of the Continental Congress (1774–1776). Hopkins signed the Declaration of Independence.

Matilda Sissieretta Joyner Jones (1869–1933) was a singer who studied music in Providence for many years. In 1892 Jones performed at the White House for President Benjamin Harrison. That same year, Jones became the first African American to sing at New York's Carnegie Hall.

Napoleon "Larry" Lajoie (1874–1959) has been called baseball's most graceful infielder. The second baseman from Woonsocket played for Philadelphia and Cleveland. In 1937 he became the sixth player to be elected to the National Baseball Hall of Fame.

Ida Lewis (1842–1911) began working as a teenager as the light-house keeper on Lime Rock in Newport Harbor. During her 50 years on the job, Lewis rescued at least 18 people from drowning. Her deeds gained her worldwide fame and a medal from President Ulysses S. Grant.

Princess Red Wing (1896–1987) was an activist who helped Narragansett Indians in Rhode Island to renew faith in their culture. Red Wing founded the Tomquag Indian Memorial Museum at Arcadia Village in Exeter. As a representative of her tribe, she addressed the United Nations.

Samuel Slater (1768–1835) is considered the founder of the cotton industry in the United States. Born in England, Slater was an apprentice to the inventor of a cotton-spinning machine that could produce thread faster than a spinning wheel. Slater moved to Pawtucket, Rhode Island, reproduced the machine, and became part owner of Slater Mill, the first successful spinning mill in the United States.

Samuel Slater

Sherwood Spring (born 1944), an astronaut, has flown on several space-shuttle voyages, supervising the experiments performed on each mission. Spring makes his home in Harmony, Rhode Island.

Sherwood Spring

Gilbert Stuart (1755–1828) was an artist who became famous for the portraits he painted of U.S. presidents and other famous people. His portrait of George Washington appears on the one-dollar bill. Stuart was born in North Kingstown, Rhode Island.

Gilbert Stuart

Stephen Wilcox Jr. (1830–1893), an inventor from Westerly, developed a water tube steam boiler that allowed a safer and better production of steam. He later co-founded the Babcock & Wilcox Company, whose products eventually led to the development of power plants for electricity production.

Leonard Woodcock (1911–2001) was a diplomat and labor union leader. From 1970 to 1977, Woodcock was president of one of the largest labor unions in the United States, the United Automobile Workers. He went on to serve as U.S. ambassador to China from 1979 to 1981. Woodcock was born in Providence.

Stephen Wilcox Jr.

FACTS-AT-A-GLANCE

Nickname: Ocean State

Song: "Rhode Island It's for Me"

Motto: Hope

Flower: violet

Tree: red maple

Bird: Rhode Island Red

Shell: quahog

Fish: striped bass

Fruit: Rhode Island greening apple

Mineral: bowenite

Date and ranking of statehood:
   May 29, 1790, the 13th state

Capital: Providence

Area: 1,045 square miles

Rank in area, nationwide: 50th

Average January temperature: 29° F

Average July temperature: 71° F

The state flag of Rhode Island features 13 stars around an anchor. The stars represent the original 13 colonies, and the anchor is a symbol of hope, the state's motto.

POPULATION GROWTH

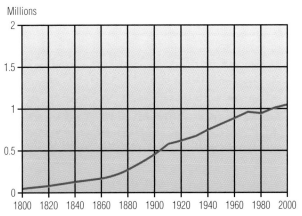

Millions

This chart shows how Rhode Island's population has grown from 1800 to 2000.

Rhode Island's state seal was adopted in 1896. The anchor symbolizes hope, and the date 1636 is the year Roger Williams founded Providence.

Population: 1,048,319 (2000 census)

Rank in population, nationwide: 43rd

Major cities and populations: (2000 census) Providence (173,618), Warwick (85,808), Cranston (79,269), Pawtucket (72,958)

U.S. senators: 2

U.S. representatives: 2

Electoral votes: 4

Natural resources: forests, granite, limestone, sand and gravel, sandstone, soil, water

Agricultural products: apples, eggs, hay, milk, potatoes, poultry, shrubs, sod, trees

Fishing: anglerfish, bluefin tuna, clams, cod, flounder, lobster, menhaden, quahogs, scallops, striped bass, yellowfish

Manufactured goods: electrical equipment, jewelry, machinery, metal products, scientific equipment, silverware

WHERE RHODE ISLANDERS WORK

Services—67 percent (services includes
jobs in trade; community, social,
and personal services; finance,
insurance, and real estate;
transportation, communication,
and utilities)

Manufacturing—15 percent

Government—13 percent

Construction—4 percent

Agriculture—1 percent

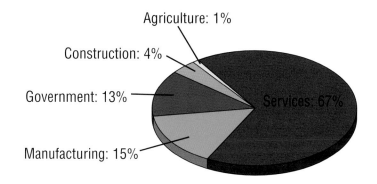

Agriculture: 1%

Construction: 4%

Government: 13%

Manufacturing: 15%

Services: 67%

GROSS STATE PRODUCT

Services—66 percent

Manufacturing—17 percent

Government—12 percent

Construction—4 percent

Agriculture—1 percent

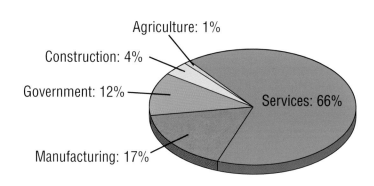

Agriculture: 1%

Construction: 4%

Government: 12%

Manufacturing: 17%

Services: 66%

STATE WILDLIFE

Mammals: deer, fox, humpback whale, mink, muskrat, otter, rabbit, raccoon, right whale, squirrel

Birds: American bittern, bald eagle, barred owl, blue jay, catbird, flicker, gull, loon, osprey, partridge, pheasant, quail, robin, ruffed grouse, screech owl, tern, wild duck, wild turkey, woodcock

Amphibians and reptiles: box turtle, eastern American toad, eastern ribbon snake, leatherback turtle, northern water snake, Ridley sea turtle, spotted salamander, wood frog

Fish: bass, bluefish, butterfish, eel, flounder, mackerel, menhaden, perch, pickerel, sea bass, striped bass, swordfish, trout, tuna

Trees: ash, birch, cedar, elm, hickory, oak, pine, poplar, red maple, willow

Wild plants: aster, cattail, dogwood, mountain laurel, red deer grass, rhododendron, trillium, violet, white daisy, wild carrot

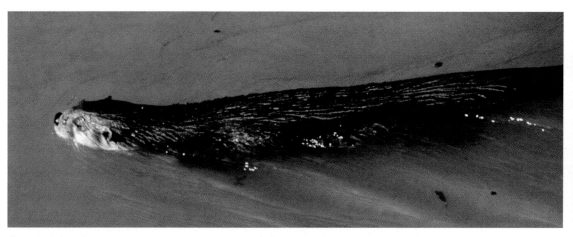

Rhode Island's ponds, rivers, and streams make perfect homes for otters.

PLACES TO VISIT

Blithewold Mansion, Gardens & Arboretum, Bristol
This 45-room mansion features more than 30 acres of landscaped grounds and gardens overlooking Narragansett Bay. The arboretum features 50,000 flowering spring bulbs, a Japanese water garden, and a giant redwood.

Block Island, southern coast
Take a ferry ride to visit the island's historic architecture. Visitors can also walk along the island's sandy beaches or check out Mohegan Bluffs, which rise 200 feet above the sea.

Green Animals Topiary Gardens, Portsmouth
See trees and shrubs sculpted into geometrical forms and animal shapes, including a teddy bear.

International Tennis Hall of Fame, Newport
Visit the oldest grass courts in America and the Tennis Hall of Fame Museum, featuring exhibits covering a century of tennis history.

Naval War College Museum, Newport
Learn more about the history of naval warfare and the naval history of Narragansett Bay.

Newport Mansions, Newport
Tour 11 mansions from America's colonial and Victorian eras. Among the most famous mansions are The Breakers, Marble House, and The Elms.

Roger Williams Park
Botanical Gardens

Roger Williams Park Botanical Gardens, Providence

This 436-acre park features exotic trees, shrubs, and flowers. The park also houses the Roger Williams Park Zoo.

Rose Island Lighthouse, Newport

Learn about the lives of lighthouse families through artifacts and photographs. Visitors can tour the lighthouse during the day and can help in the lighthouse operation at night.

Slater Mill Historic Site, Pawtucket

This historic site features Slater Mill, the first factory in America to use water-powered machines. Visitors can also see the Sylvanus Brown House, Wilkinson Mill, and reconstructed 16,000-pound water wheel.

South County Museum, Wickford

Learn more about the rural and maritime heritage of southern Rhode Island through the museum's collection of more than 20,000 artifacts.

ANNUAL EVENTS

Rose Island Seal Watching Tours, Newport—*March*

May Breakfasts, statewide—*April–May*

WaterFire Providence, Providence—*May–November*

Festival of Historic Houses, Providence—*June*

Gaspee Days Parade, Warwick—*June*

Black Ships Festival, Newport—*July*

Hall of Fame Tennis Championships, Newport—*July*

Wickford Art Festival, North Kingston—*July*

JVC Jazz Festival, Newport—*August*

International Quahog Festival, Wickford—*August*

Tuna Tournament, near Narragansett and Galilee—*September*

Autumnfest, Woonsocket—*October*

Scituate Art Festival, Scituate—*October*

LEARN MORE ABOUT RHODE ISLAND

BOOKS

General

Heinrichs, Ann. *Rhode Island.* Chicago: Children's Press, 1990.

Klein, Ted. *Rhode Island.* New York: Benchmark Books, 1998. For older readers.

McNair, Sylvia. *Rhode Island.* New York: Children's Press, 2000. For older readers.

Special Interest

Gaustad, Edwin S. *Roger Williams: Prophet of Liberty.* New York: Oxford University Press Children's Books, 2001. Historical account of Williams's experiences in the New World, including his efforts to establish the colony that eventually became Rhode Island.

Koller, Jackie French. *Nickommoh: A Thanksgiving Celebration.* New York: Atheneum, 1999. Exploration of the Narragansett Indians' traditional Nickommoh feast, a gathering similar to modern-day Thanksgiving.

MacAulay, David. *Mill.* Boston: Houghton Mifflin Company, 1989. A look back at New England's mills in the 1800s, including the planning, construction, and operation. The book also explains how the mill was important to a community's economic and social life.

Schlesinger, Arthur M. *Anne Hutchinson: Religious Leader.* Philadelphia: Chelsea House Publishing, 2000. This biography covers the life of the woman who was banished from the Massachusetts Bay Colony for her religious beliefs and who later settled on Aquidneck Island.

Weinstein-Farson, Laurie. *The Wampanoag.* New York: Chelsea House, 1991. An in-depth look at the Wampanoag Indians, their customs, history, and recent events.

Fiction

Curtis, Alice Turner. *Little Maid of Narragansett Bay.* Bedford, MA: Applewood Books, 1998. Eleven-year-old Penelope Balfourd lives on a farm in Rhode Island during the Revolutionary War. When her father goes off to fight, Penelope decides she too must do something to help the American army.

Lisle, Janet Taylor. *The Art of Keeping Cool.* New York: Atheneum, 2000. Robert and his family move to Rhode Island to live with his grandparents during World War II. But the family's problems soon prove to be as difficult as the war. For older readers.

Nicholson, Peggy. *The Case of the Furtive Firebug.* Minneapolis, MN: Lerner Publications Company, 1995. Hally Watkins needs all the help she can get to prove that her friend is not responsible for setting a house fire in Newport, Rhode Island.

WEBSITES

Rhode Island Online
<http://www.state.ri.us/>
Learn more about Little Rhody through the state's official website. It has information about the state's history, fun facts, and government.

Visit Rhode Island
<http://www.visitrhodeisland.com>
The state's official tourism website has information about sites and events in the Ocean State.

The Providence Journal
<http://www.projo.com/>
The online version of Rhode Island's largest newspaper features local and national news, plus information about living and working in the Ocean State.

Greenwich Bay
<http://www.seagrant.gso.uri.edu/G_Bay>
Learn more about the plants and animals of Rhode Island's Greenwich Bay, an estuary in Narragansett Bay.

PRONUNCIATION GUIDE

Aquidneck (uh-KWIHD-nehk)

Conanicut (kuh-NAN-ih-kuht)

Narragansett (nar-uh-GAN-suht)

Nipmuc (NIP-muhk)

Pequot (PEE-kwaht)

Sakonnet (suh-KAHN-uht)

Scituate (SICH-uh-wuht)

Seekonk (SEE-kahngk)

Verrazzano, Giovanni da (veh-raht-SAHN-oh, joh-VAHN-nee dah)

Wampanoag (wahm-puh-NOH-ag)

Warwick Light on Narragansett Bay serves as a U.S. Coast Guard station.

GLOSSARY

charter: a written statement from the governing power of a territory that guarantees its citizens certain rights and that defines the official boundaries of the territory

colony: a territory ruled by a country some distance away

combined sewer: a system of underground pipes that carries both sewage and storm water

glacier: a large body of ice and snow that moves slowly over land

immigrant: a person who moves into a foreign country and settles there

Industrial Revolution: the change from making products by hand, often at home, to using water-powered machinery, usually in factories. Powered equipment made it possible for goods to be made quickly, cheaply, and in large quantities. The revolution in the United States began in the late 1700s.

lagoon: a shallow lake or pond, especially one that joins a larger body of water

moraine: a mass of sand, gravel, and rocks, which is pushed along or left behind by a glacier

precipitation: rain, snow, and other forms of moisture that fall to earth

reservation: public land set aside by the government to be used by Native Americans

reservoir: a place where water is collected and stored for later use

wastewater: water that carries waste, or sewage, from homes, businesses, and industries

INDEX

PHOTO ACKNOWLEDGMENTS

Cover photographs by © Kevin Fleming/CORBIS (left) and © Onne van der Wal/ CORBIS (right); PresentationMaps.com, pp. 1, 8, 9, 48; © Jeff Greenberg/Visuals Unlimited, pp. 2–3; © Rob & Ann Simpson/Visuals Unlimited, p. 3; © Roger Cole/Visuals Unlimited, pp. 4 (detail), 7 (detail), 10, 13, 15, 17 (detail), 18, 37, 39 (detail), 52 (detail), 54; Courtesy of Providence Warwick Convention and Visitors Bureau, pp. 6, 39, 40, 41, 75, 80; R. De Goursey/Visuals Unlimited, p. 11; Jeff Greenberg, pp. 12, 42, 43, 45; Jim Simondet, p. 14; Ron Spomer/Visuals Unlimited, p. 16 (left); Blackstone Valley Tourism Council, Lincoln, Rhode Island, p. 16 (right); Rhode Island Historical Society, pp. 17, 20, 21, 23, 24, 26, 30, 33, 68 (second from bottom); Newport Convention & Visitors Bureau, pp. 19, 44 (both); Library of Congress, p. 22; Dictionary of American Portraits, pp. 25, 29 (top), 66 (second from top), 67 (second from top, second from bottom), 68 (second from top), 69 (top, second from bottom, bottom); Independent Picture Service, p. 27, 68 (top); Doyen Salsig, p. 28; Independence National Historical Park Collection, p. 29 (bottom); Slater Mill Historic Site, Pawtucket, Rhode Island, pp. 31, 32; © Barbara Laatsch-Hupp/LAATSCH-HUPP PHOTO, pp. 34, 47; From the Collection of the Newport Historical Society (P164), p. 35; From the Collection of the Newport Historical Society (P133), p. 36; Thomas P. Benincas, Jr., p. 38; © AP/Wide World Photos, p. 46; Rhode Island Division of Agriculture, p. 49 (both); Erwin C. "Bud" Nielsen, p. 50; © Gerry Lemmo, p. 51; Bruce Eastman, R.I. Shellfisherman's Association, p. 52; Jamal Kadri, Save the Bay, pp. 53, 56, 57; © Joseph L. Fontenot/Visuals Unlimited, p. 55; Save the Bay, pp. 58, 59; Toby Schnobrich, p. 60; William J. Weber/Visuals Unlimited, p. 61; Tim Seeley, pp. 63, 71 (top), 72; Franklin D. Roosevelt Library, p. 66 (top); Hollywood Book & Poster, Inc., pp. 66 (second from bottom), 67 (top); © Bettmann/CORBIS, p. 66 (bottom); © Mitchell Gerber/COR-BIS, p. 67 (bottom); Providence Journal-Bulletin, p. 68 (bottom); NASA, p. 69 (second from top); Jean Matheny, p. 70; NOAA National Estuarine Research Reserve Collection, p. 73.